DATE DUE
Fecha Para Retornar

			PRINTED IN U.S.A.

Yosemite

National Park

by Grace Hansen

Abdo

NATIONAL PARKS

Kids

Yosemite National Park

Yosemite National Park

is in Northern California.

It is very beautiful.

Yosemite

National Park

by Grace Hansen

Abdo
NATIONAL PARKS
Kids

abdopublishing.com

Published by Abdo Kids, a division of ABDO, P.O. Box 398166, Minneapolis, Minnesota 55439.
Copyright © 2018 by Abdo Consulting Group, Inc. International copyrights reserved in all countries.
No part of this book may be reproduced in any form without written permission from the publisher.
Abdo Kids Jumbo™ is a trademark and logo of Abdo Kids.

Printed in the United States of America, North Mankato, Minnesota.

102017

012018

 THIS BOOK CONTAINS RECYCLED MATERIALS

Photo Credits: Alamy, iStock, Library of Congress, Shutterstock

Production Contributors: Teddy Borth, Jennie Forsberg, Grace Hansen

Design Contributors: Dorothy Toth, Laura Mitchell

Publisher's Cataloging in Publication Data

Names: Hansen, Grace, author.
Title: Yosemite National Park / by Grace Hansen.
Description: Minneapolis, Minnesota : Abdo Kids, 2018. | Series: National Parks |
    Includes glossary, index and online resource (page 24).
Identifiers: LCCN 2017943272 | ISBN 9781532104374 (lib.bdg.) | ISBN 9781532105494 (ebook) |
    ISBN 9781532106057 (Read-to-me ebook)
Subjects: LCSH: Yosemite National Park (Calif.)--Juvenile literature. | California--Yosemite National Park--
    Juvenile literature. |National parks and reserves--Juvenile literature.
Classification: DDC 917.94--dc23
LC record available at https://lccn.loc.gov/2017943272

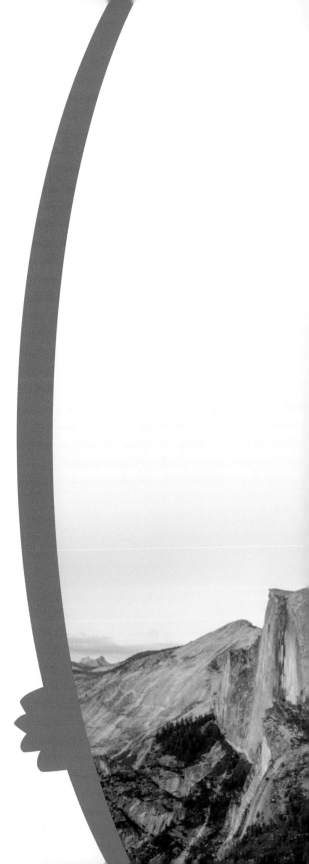

Table of Contents

Yosemite National Park

Yosemite National Park

is in Northern California.

It is very beautiful.

5

Naturalist John Muir worked hard to protect the land. President Abraham Lincoln set aside the land in 1864. It became a national park on October 1, 1890.

Climate

The park is almost 1,200 square miles (3,108 km^2) in size. It is mostly covered in snow between November and May. It is warmer in the summer. Many plants grow.

Habitats

Granite cliffs make up much of

Yosemite's **geology**. Half Dome

and El Capitan are well known.

Both are in Yosemite Valley.

Yosemite Valley is known for its waterfalls. Wildflowers grow in its meadows. It is common to spot mule deer there.

13

Meadows are found at many **elevations** in the park. They are important to lots of animals. They provide food and water.

15

Forests are also at nearly every **elevation**. Many types of trees grow at 3,000 feet (914.4 m). Animals like black bears live in these forests.

Plants like lichens can grow above 9,500 feet (2,895.6 m). Whitebark pine, a special tree, can grow at this elevation. Mountain lions roam these areas of the park.

19

Yosemite has many rivers and streams. Fish are only **native** to the waters at lower **elevations**. Many fish live in the Merced River.

Index

Abdo Kids ONLINE
FREE! ONLINE MULTIMEDIA RESOURCES

Visit **abdokids.com** and use this code to access crafts, games, videos, and more!

Abdo Kids Code:
NYK4374

24